EVERYBODY LOVES RAMEN

Recipes, Stories, Games, and Fun Facts About the Noodles You Love

ERIC HITES

Andrews McMeel Publishing®

a division of Andrews McMeel Universal

I dedicate this book to Darby Myers, my best friend, and his family, Phil, Arlene, Misty, and Kiley. I will miss you always.

I also want to thank my family, Mom, Dad, and my brother, Chris. You were all a great help to me and helped me get this project done.

I thank Heather for spurring me to get this book started and George for helping get my first copies made. Also a special thanks to Ryves Hall Youth Center and its director for giving me experience and a leg up when I was in school. I will never forget the days of scavenging the food pantry to feed the children of the center.

And I want to thank my wife Angie for giving me the strength to start my journey, which led to the rebirth of this edition.

Contents

The Grand Introduction . . . **ix**

What You're Gonna Need (Just the Basics) . . . **xi**

What You're Gonna Need (In Reality) . . . **xiii**

The Gobble Gobble Asian Noodle Delight . . . **2**

Stroganoff Ramen-Style . . . **4**

What's Up, Doc? Ramen Pancakes . . . **6**

Upstream Salmon Ramen . . . **8**

911 Heart Attack Ramen . . . **10**

Cheesy Ramen[3] . . . **14**

Chili Cheese Dip à La Ramen . . . **16**

Fourth o' July Confetti Bean Salad . . . **18**

Cow and Chicken Surprise . . . **20**

Flaming Poultry and Peanuts . . . **22**

Creamy Ramen Mushroom Soup . . . **26**

Wanna-Be Italian Ramen . . . **28**

A Vegetarian's Slipup . . . **30**

Chili Fish Ramen . . . **34**

Ramen Pizza Party . . . **36**

Zesty Ramen Omelets . . . **38**

Chicken in Gravy over Ramen . . . **40**

Popeye Cashew Ramen . . . **44**

Easy Cheesy Ramen . . . **46**

Fit-for-a-King Salad . . . **48**

Four-Alarm Fish Ramen . . . **50**

Orange "PEZ" Chicken Soup . . . **54**

Thai-One-On Ramen . . . **56**

Rip-Roaring Ramen Chili . . . **58**

Odds-and-Ends Hearty Ramen Soup . . . **62**

Hawaiian Chicken Ramen . . . **64**

Big Shrimp Omelets . . . **66**

Rootin' Tootin' Ramen Chili . . . **68**

Cholesterol-Killer Ramen . . . **70**

Elvis's Fav' Gravy Ramen . . . **74**

Porky's Stir-Fry . . . **76**

Top-Speed 3-Minute Ramen . . . **78**

Crabby Spinach Ramen . . . **80**

Ramen Cookie Delight . . . **82**

Pseudo Szechwan Ramen . . . **84**

Saturday Brunch Ramen . . . **86**

Kickin' Dduk-Boki . . . **90**

Hog 'n' Cheese Mix and Melt . . . **92**

Poppin' Broccoli Slaw . . . **94**

Buttery Sesame Ramen . . . **96**

Cheap-as-It-Gets Ramen Salad . . . **98**

Death Valley Treat . . . **100**

Florentine à la Polo and Newman . . . **104**

Hijacked Taco Bell Ramen . . . **106**

Super Pregnancy Ramen . . . **108**

Custom Kimche Ramen-Style . . . **112**

Super Ramen Burritos . . . **114**

Red-Nosed Ramen . . . **118**

La Chico's Hearty Soup . . . **120**

Vegetarian's Power Dish . . . **122**

The Grand Introduction

Thank you for reading *Everybody Loves Ramen*. Being on a budget, I know what it is like to cook for yourself while trying to make ends meet. We all know ramen noodles are a staple in the pantries of many single Americans. I have written this book to help you learn creative new ways to prepare these wonderful noodles and document your noodle memories.

Inside I will not only show you the different ways you can prepare and serve ramen noodles, I will also give you ways to document the very special memories you will create as you prepare and share your feast.

So get that water boiling, crack open this book, and start a new phase in your life that I call the Ramen Noodle Years.

Your Noodle Guru,
Eric Hites

What You're Gonna Need

(Just the Basics)

Bowl and/or pot

Water

Ramen noodles

Eating utensil

Fair amount of hunger

Like I said, it's just the basics.

What You're Gonna Need

(In Reality)

PREPARATION

One stainless steel
chef's knife

One paring knife

Vegetable peeler

Cheese slicer/grater

Cutting board

Can opener

Kitchen shears

Bottle opener

MIXING AND MEASURING

Measuring spoon set

Mixing bowls

Wide spatula
(metal or plastic)

Measuring cup
(1- and 2-cup size)

Dry measure cup set

Wire wisk

Rubber spatula

Wooden spoons

OTHER UTENSILS

Colander
(noodle drainer)

Nonstick skillet

2-quart saucepan
with cover

Flat cookie sheet

EVERYBODY
LOVES
RAN

MEN

The Gobble Gobble Asian Noodle Delight

1¼ pounds ground turkey

2 packages ramen noodles (oriental flavor), seasoning packets removed and set aside

2 cups water

1½ cups cut-up broccoli

½ cup sliced carrots

1 can sliced water chestnuts

¼ teaspoon grated ginger

¼ cup cut-up green onions

1 In a large skillet, brown the ground turkey over medium heat for 10 to 12 minutes, breaking the meat up into pieces.

2 Pour off the drippings.

3 Season the meat with the contents of one of the reserved seasoning packets. Remove the meat from the skillet. Set aside.

4 In same skillet, combine the water, broccoli, carrots, water chestnuts, two packages of ramen noodles (broken up), ginger, and the remaining seasoning packet.

5 Bring to a boil and reduce the heat to low.

6 Cover and simmer 3 minutes or until the noodles are tender, stirring occasionally.

7 Return the turkey to the skillet, and stir in the green onions.

8 Mix well, and serve.

WHAT YOU'RE GONNA DO!

When did you serve this dish for the first time?

_____

_____

Did you share the dish?

_____

_____

Whom did you share it with?

_____

_____

What was the occasion?

_____

_____

What did you serve with it?

_____

_____

Any special memories of the dish/activities?

_____

_____

How would you rate this dish?

_____

_____

Comments:

_____

_____

Stroganoff Ramen-Style

⅔ cup water

2 tablespoons flour

3 ounces beef (just about any kind will work, even lean hamburger)

2½ tablespoons margarine

1 cup canned mushrooms (optional)

1 package ramen noodles (beef flavor), seasoning packet removed and set aside

2 tablespoons sour cream, or more if needed

1 Mix ¼ cup of water with the flour. Set aside.

2 In a small saucepan, cook the meat with ½ tablespoon of the margarine until the meat is no longer pink.

3 Add 1 cup mushrooms, if desired.

4 Add the remaining water and the contents of the reserved beef seasoning packet to the pan.

5 Let this cook for 2 minutes.

6 Cook the noodles according to package directions. Drain well. Set aside.

7 Pour the flour-water mixture into the boiling beef/water/seasoning.

8 The mixture will thicken almost immediately. Be careful!

9 Add the sour cream; stir until the mixture is smooth.

10 If it is still too thick add a little more sour cream; if too runny add more flour-water.

11 Add the remaining 2 tablespoons of margarine to the noodles and stir.

12 Put on a plate, pour the mock Stroganoff over the noodles, and serve.

WHAT YOU'RE GONNA DO!

When did you serve this dish for the first time?

_____

_____

Did you share the dish?

_____

_____

Whom did you share it with?

_____

_____

What was the occasion?

_____

_____

What did you serve with it?

_____

_____

Any special memories of the dish/activities?

_____

_____

How would you rate this dish?

_____

_____

Comments:

_____

_____

What's Up, Doc? Ramen Pancakes

1 carrot

1 package ramen noodles, seasoning packet removed

1 cup grated cheddar cheese

3 tablespoons butter

Cracked pepper

Garnish

1 Grate the carrot with a cheese grater.

2 Cook the noodles according to package directions. Drain well.

3 Toss the noodles, carrot, and cheese together in a bowl.

4 Melt the butter in a frying pan.

5 Shape the mixture into small pancake-like patties.

6 Fry the patties till browned lightly on each side.

7 Serve with the cracked pepper and garnish.

WHAT YOU'RE GONNA DO!

When did you serve this dish for the first time?

_____

_____

Did you share the dish?

_____

_____

Whom did you share it with?

_____

_____

What was the occasion?

_____

_____

What did you serve with it?

_____

_____

Any special memories of the dish/activities?

_____

_____

How would you rate this dish?

_____

_____

Comments:

_____

_____

Upstream Salmon Ramen

1 tablespoon butter

1 onion, finely chopped

1½ cups milk

4 ounces cream cheese, cubed

2 packages ramen noodles (oriental flavor), seasoning packets removed and set aside

1 cup julienned carrots

1 cup julienned zucchini

2 cans (6.5 ounces each) salmon, drained and broken into chunks

1 Heat the butter in a skillet.

2 Add the chopped onion.

3 Sauté the onion for 2 minutes.

4 Add the milk, cream cheese, and the contents of one of the reserved seasoning packets.

5 Cook on medium heat until the mixture is smooth, stirring while cooking. *Do not boil.*

6 Add the carrots, zucchini, and salmon; simmer for 5 minutes.

7 Cook the noodles with the contents of the remaining seasoning packet according to package directions for 3 minutes. Drain well.

8 Add the ramen noodles to the salmon and vegetable mixture.

9 Toss gently and serve immediately.

WHAT YOU'RE GONNA DO!

When did you serve this dish for the first time?

_____

_____

Did you share the dish?

_____

_____

Whom did you share it with?

_____

_____

What was the occasion?

_____

_____

What did you serve with it?

_____

_____

Any special memories of the dish/activities?

_____

_____

How would you rate this dish?

_____

_____

Comments:

_____

_____

9ll Heart Attack Ramen

2 cups water

1 small onion, diced into semi-large chunks

¼ can Spam, sliced

1 package ramen noodles (any kind), seasoning packet removed and set aside

1 egg, beaten

¼ cup shredded mozzarella cheese

10

1 Bring the water to a boil in a medium pot.

2 Add the onion and sliced Spam.

3 Add the contents of the reserved seasoning packet.

4 Continue to cook until the onions become soft.

5 Add the noodles and egg slowly.

6 Cook until the noodles are done.

7 Stir in the cheese and serve.

WHAT YOU'RE GONNA DO!

When did you serve this dish for the first time?

_____

_____

Did you share the dish?

_____

_____

Whom did you share it with?

_____

_____

What was the occasion?

_____

_____

What did you serve with it?

_____

_____

Any special memories of the dish/activities?

_____

_____

How would you rate this dish?

_____

_____

Comments:

_____

_____

Your new life motto:

"YA GOT TO LOVE A MEAT THAT COMES IN A CAN."

RAMEN
FACTOIDS
ALERT
Nº 1

One pound of ramen
noodles weighs the same
as one pound of gold.

But you can't eat gold.

Cheesy Ramen[3]

SERVES 1

1 package ramen noodles (any flavor)

1 egg, beaten

1 slice American cheese

1 tablespoon bacon bits

1 Preheat the broiler.

2 Cook the noodles according to package instructions, but do not destroy the cube-like shape of the noodles.

3 Once the noodles start to soften, carefully pour the egg on top of the cube.

4 When the egg is cooked, gently scoop out the cube with a spatula.

5 Quickly cover the noodle–egg cube with the slice of American cheese.

6 Sprinkle the bacon bits on top of the cheese.

7 Place the whole cube on a cookie sheet.

8 Put the sheet on the top shelf of the oven and let the cube broil until cheese melts. Watch carefully.

9 Remove from the heat and serve.

WHAT YOU'RE GONNA DO!

When did you serve this dish for the first time?

_____

_____

Did you share the dish?

_____

_____

Whom did you share it with?

_____

_____

What was the occasion?

_____

_____

What did you serve with it?

_____

_____

Any special memories of the dish/activities?

_____

_____

How would you rate this dish?

_____

_____

Comments:

_____

_____

Chili Cheese Dip à La Ramen

1 package ramen noodles (beef flavor)

1 can chili with beans, average size

16 ounces sour cream

2 cups shredded Cheddar cheese

2 cups shredded mozzarella cheese

1 Break the noodles into very small pieces.

2 Cook the noodles according to package directions. Drain well.

3 Add the noodles, chili, sour cream, Cheddar, and mozzarella to a microwave-safe bowl.

4 Mix well.

5 Heat in the microwave, stopping to stir frequently, until the cheese is melted.

6 Serve with tortilla chips.

Note: Makes a great party dish.

WHAT YOU'RE GONNA DO!

When did you serve this dish for the first time?

_____

_____

Did you share the dish?

_____

_____

Whom did you share it with?

_____

_____

What was the occasion?

_____

_____

What did you serve with it?

_____

_____

Any special memories of the dish/activities?

_____

_____

How would you rate this dish?

_____

_____

Comments:

_____

_____

Fourth o' July Confetti Bean Salad

SERVES 4

1 package ramen noodles (chicken flavor), seasoning packet removed and set aside

1 cup drained cooked or canned red, pinto, or pink beans

½ cup low-fat mayonnaise

¼ cup chopped green pepper

¼ cup chopped celery

¼ cup chopped carrot

¼ cup chopped green onion

2 tablespoons diced sweet pickles

2 tablespoons toasted pine nuts

Fresh spinach leaves

Pickle wedges and carrot curls for garnish

1 Cook the noodles according to package directions. Drain well and cool to room temperature.

2 In medium mixing bowl, combine the cooked ramen noodles with the beans, mayonnaise, green pepper, celery, carrot, green onion, pickles, and pine nuts. Toss the mixture to combine.

3 Sprinkle the contents of the reserved seasoning packet over the tossed mixture and toss again.

4 Cover and refrigerate the salad until it is well chilled.

5 To serve, spoon the mixture onto the spinach leaves and garnish.

WHAT YOU'RE GONNA DO!

When did you serve this dish for the first time?

_____

_____

Did you share the dish?

_____

_____

Whom did you share it with?

_____

_____

What was the occasion?

_____

_____

What did you serve with it?

_____

_____

Any special memories of the dish/activities?

_____

_____

How would you rate this dish?

_____

_____

Comments:

_____

_____

Cow and Chicken Surprise

2 packages ramen noodles (chicken flavor), seasoning packets removed and set aside

2 cups milk

1 diced tomato

1 diced green onion, for garnish

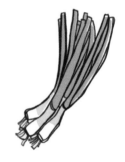

1 Cook the noodles according to package directions. Drain well.

2 Place the noodles in a medium bowl.

3 In a saucepan, combine the milk, diced tomato, and contents of the reserved seasoning packets.

4 Simmer the milk and tomato mixture until it has a creamy texture.

5 Add the milk mixture to the noodles.

6 Garnish with the green onion, and serve.

WHAT YOU'RE GONNA DO!

When did you serve this dish for the first time?

_____

_____

Did you share the dish?

_____

_____

Whom did you share it with?

_____

_____

What was the occasion?

_____

_____

What did you serve with it?

_____

_____

Any special memories of the dish/activities?

_____

_____

How would you rate this dish?

_____

_____

Comments:

_____

_____

Flaming Poultry and Peanuts

2 packages ramen noodles (chicken sesame flavor), seasoning packets and oil seasoning removed and set aside

1 cup peanut butter

4 tablespoons rice or wine vinegar

3 tablespoons soy sauce

2 garlic cloves, crushed

¼ teaspoon red pepper sauce or cayenne pepper

3 cups broccoli florets and thinly sliced stems

1 cup frozen peas

6 cups boiling water

1 red bell pepper, halved and cut into thin strips

2 cups cubed cooked chicken (optional)

2 green onions, thinly sliced

1 In a small bowl, whisk together the peanut butter, vinegar, soy sauce, garlic, hot pepper sauce, and contents of the oil seasoning packets until smooth.

2 Set aside.

3 Place the broccoli and peas in the boiling water.

4 Cook 2 minutes. Add the noodles, the contents of both reserved seasoning packets, and the peanut mixture.

5 Boil for 2 additional minutes.

6 Add the bell pepper and chicken.

7 Cook for 1½ minutes.

8 Garnish with the green onions and serve.

WHAT YOU'RE GONNA DO!

When did you serve this dish for the first time?

_____

_____

Did you share the dish?

_____

_____

Whom did you share it with?

_____

_____

What was the occasion?

_____

_____

What did you serve with it?

_____

_____

Any special memories of the dish/activities?

_____

_____

How would you rate this dish?

_____

_____

Comments:

_____

_____

RAMEN
LORE

My friends used to make fun of me because I ate "smack"-brand ramen. I bought my ramen at ACO Hardware, on sale for $.10 a pop. It's some of the best ramen I ever had. My daily ritual was to sit down with a double bowl of ramen and my girlfriend and a Scrabble board. Smack-brand ramen . . . the noodles of romance.

–K. ZUBON

RAMEN
LORE

Well, a friend and I used to eat ramen as the "official food" for watching movies. Apparently someone thought it was funny to call it "Raw Men." So we did, and to this day refer to it as "Raw Men."

–SHERILL K.

Creamy Ramen Mushroom Soup

3 tablespoons butter

1 garlic clove, minced

½ cup chopped onion

2 cups sliced raw mushrooms, your favorite type

1 cup water

¼ teaspoon thyme

1 cup light cream

1 package ramen noodles (chicken mushroom flavor), seasoning packet removed and set aside

1 tablespoon chopped fresh parsley

1 Melt the butter in a pot over medium-low heat.

2 Add the garlic, onion, and mushrooms to the pot.

3 Sauté until the onions are clear and the mushrooms are soft.

4 Add the water, thyme, and the contents of the reserved seasoning packet to the pot.

5 Stir in the light cream.

6 Cook over low heat until warm. Do not boil.

7 Break up the noodles and add them to the pot.

8 Simmer for 5 minutes.

9 Stir in the parsley and serve.

WHAT YOU'RE GONNA DO!

When did you serve this dish for the first time?

_____

_____

Did you share the dish?

_____

_____

Whom did you share it with?

_____

_____

What was the occasion?

_____

_____

What did you serve with it?

_____

_____

Any special memories of the dish/activities?

_____

_____

How would you rate this dish?

_____

_____

Comments:

_____

_____

Wanna-Be Italian Ramen

1 package ramen noodles, seasoning packet removed

2 tablespoons olive oil

½ cup grated or shredded Parmesan cheese, or more to taste

Chopped garlic, herbs, and/or spices, to taste

1 Cook the noodles according to package directions, leaving out the seasoning packet. Drain well.

2 Add the olive oil so that noodles are slick and coated.

3 Add ½ cup Parmesan cheese, or more.

4 Add the chopped garlic and/or herbs.

5 Stir well and serve.

WHAT YOU'RE GONNA DO!

When did you serve this dish for the first time?

_____

_____

Did you share the dish?

_____

_____

Whom did you share it with?

_____

_____

What was the occasion?

_____

_____

What did you serve with it?

_____

_____

Any special memories of the dish/activities?

_____

_____

How would you rate this dish?

_____

_____

Comments:

_____

_____

A Vegetarian's Slipup

(Hey, at least it's still a salad)

1 package ramen noodles (oriental flavor), broken up, seasoning packet removed and set aside

1 cup fresh spinach, shredded

½ cup thinly sliced red onion

½ pound deli roast beef, sliced into bite-sized strips

2 tablespoons rice vinegar

2 tablespoons canola oil

1 tablespoon prepared horseradish

¼ cup drained julienned pickled beets

1 teaspoon poppy seeds

1 Cook the noodles according to package directions. Drain well.

2 Combine with the spinach, onion, and roast beef in a serving bowl.

3 Mix the contents of the reserved seasoning packet with the vinegar, oil, and horseradish.

4 Pour the mixture over the noodles and toss.

5 Sprinkle in the beets and poppy seeds and serve at room temperature.

WHAT YOU'RE GONNA DO!

When did you serve this dish for the first time?

_____

_____

Did you share the dish?

_____

_____

Whom did you share it with?

_____

_____

What was the occasion?

_____

_____

What did you serve with it?

_____

_____

Any special memories of the dish/activities?

_____

_____

How would you rate this dish?

_____

_____

Comments:

_____

_____

RAMEN
FACTOIDS
ALERT
№ 2

A 160-pound person is equal in weight
to 853.3 typical packages of
ramen noodles.

If you ate one package per day,
you could eat your weight in
ramen noodles in 2.34 years.

RAMEN
LORE

My friend at UCLA tapped the dorm's hot water line and put a filter and some coils on it to get instant hot water for ramen noodles.

—DARBY M.

I used to love ramen when I was in my late teens and early twenties. Heck, I still love it and I'm now in my thirties. My favorite standby with them is a can of creamy soup, two cans of water, a packet of noodles. Take to a boil, then add frozen veggies.

—KINYA K.

Chili Fish Ramen

1 pound any type seafish, cleaned, chopped, salted, and soured

Garlic to taste

2 (15-ounce) cans mixed vegetables, drained

Parsley branches

4 shiitakes and/or other mushrooms, no champignons

1 scallion, chopped

Chili tofu

3 cups water

½ package frozen mixed seafood, washed in hot water and drained

3 packages ramen noodles (1 chicken flavor and 2 hot and spicy flavor), seasoning packets removed and set aside

1 large package imitation crabmeat, chopped

6 tablespoons oyster sauce or fish sauce

Tabasco hot sauce to taste

1 teaspoon liquor (sake or Mekong brandy recommended)

Fresh parsley and/or Japanese cress

1 Put the cleaned/salted/soured fish into a pot.

2 Add the garlic, mixed vegetables, parsley branches, shiitakes, scallion, and the chili tofu.

3 Add the water, bring to a boil, and then add the noodles.

4 Simmer for 10 to 20 minutes, then remove the parsley branches and discard.

5 Add the frozen mixed seafood.

6 Simmer for 5 minutes.

7 Add the contents of the reserved seasoning packets and stir gently; add the imitation crabmeat and oyster/fish sauce, still stirring.

8 Add the hot sauce.

9 Add the liquor. Divide the chili among 8 soup bowls, garnish each with some chopped parsley or Japanese cress, and serve.

Note: You can get any of the opposite listed items in any Asian market. Also, some supermarkets will have the items you need.

WHAT YOU'RE GONNA DO!

When did you serve this dish for the first time?

_____

Did you share the dish?

_____

Whom did you share it with?

_____

What was the occasion?

_____

What did you serve with it?

_____

Any special memories of the dish/activities?

_____

How would you rate this dish?

_____

Comments:

_____

Ramen Pizza Party

2 packages ramen noodles (beef flavor), seasoning packets removed and set aside

1 teaspoon salt

½ pound ground beef

½ cup chopped onion

½ cup sliced mushrooms

1 egg

½ cup milk

3 tablespoons grated Parmesan cheese

1 (15½-ounce) jar spaghetti sauce

8 ounces mozzarella cheese, grated

1 Cover a pizza pan with aluminum foil and build up the edges to form a ½-inch tall rim around the edge of the pan. Preheat the oven to 350°.

2 Cook the noodles according to package directions. Drain well.

3 Brown the beef, onion, mushrooms, and the contents of the reserved seasoning packets together; drain the excess fat and set aside.

4 Beat together the egg, milk, and Parmesan cheese, and stir into the ramen noodles.

5 Evenly spread the noodle/egg mixture onto the pizza pan.

6 Pour the spaghetti sauce over the noodles.

7 Sprinkle the reserved meat mixture over the sauce.

8 Top with the mozzarella cheese.

9 Bake for 20 minutes or until golden and bubbly brown. Remove from oven and let stand 5 minutes on counter.

10 Cut and serve.

WHAT YOU'RE GONNA DO!

When did you serve this dish for the first time?

_____

_____

Did you share the dish?

_____

_____

Whom did you share it with?

_____

_____

What was the occasion?

_____

_____

What did you serve with it?

_____

_____

Any special memories of the dish/activities?

_____

_____

How would you rate this dish?

_____

_____

Comments:

_____

_____

Zesty Ramen Omelets

1 package ramen noodles (any flavor), seasoning packet removed and set aside

1 green onion, chopped

2 eggs, beaten

1 teaspoon sesame oil

½ cup of your favorite cheese, or more to taste

Salt and freshly ground black pepper

1 Cook the noodles according to package directions. Drain well.

2 Add the contents of the reserved seasoning packet, onion, and eggs to the noodles and toss gently.

3 Add the sesame oil to a medium nonstick pan.

4 Spread the egg and noodle mixture out evenly in pan.

5 Cook on medium heat for 2 to 3 minutes.

6 Sprinkle the cheese over the top of the omelet.

7 Half-flip the omelet to make a pocket.

8 Cook over medium heat for 3 to 5 minutes on each side.

9 Salt and pepper to taste and serve.

WHAT YOU'RE GONNA DO!

When did you serve this dish for the first time?

_____

_____

Did you share the dish?

_____

_____

Whom did you share it with?

_____

_____

What was the occasion?

_____

_____

What did you serve with it?

_____

_____

Any special memories of the dish/activities?

_____

_____

How would you rate this dish?

_____

_____

Comments:

_____

_____

Chicken in Gravy over Ramen

3 ounces uncooked chicken, cut in small squares

2½ tablespoons margarine

1 package ramen noodles (chicken flavor), seasoning packet removed and set aside

½ cup water

¼ cup flour-water (¼ cup cold water and 2 tablespoons flour, mixed well), or more if needed

2 tablespoons cream, or more if needed

1 In a small saucepan, cook the chicken in ½ tablespoon of the margarine until done.

2 Stir in the contents of the reserved seasoning packet and ½ cup water.

3 Bring to a boil.

4 Add the flour water, a little at a time, stirring continuously. The mixture will thicken almost immediately, so be careful.

5 Add the cream slowly. The mixture will become smooth.

6 Heat until boiling. Remove from the heat. If the mixture is too thick add more cream; if it is too thin add more flour-water.

7 Break up the noodles and cook according to package directions. Drain well.

8 Add the rest of the margarine to the drained noodles.

9 Spoon the gravy over the noodles and serve.

WHAT YOU'RE GONNA DO!

When did you serve this dish for the first time?

_____

_____

Did you share the dish?

_____

_____

Whom did you share it with?

_____

_____

What was the occasion?

_____

_____

What did you serve with it?

_____

_____

Any special memories of the dish/activities?

_____

_____

How would you rate this dish?

_____

_____

Comments:

_____

_____

Ramen Crossword

Down

1. A legitimate complaint.
2. Pertaining to the Far East.
5. Drawn-out pasta.
6. Another name for the runt of the litter.
9. It's two parts H and one part O.
12. New Orleans, "The Big _____."

Across

1. Could be sugar or orange.
3. You may find this in the road.
4. A type of movie camera shot.
7. Which came first, this or the egg.
8. Jack be nimble and Jack be this.
10. Something you would mail or ship.
11. Not expensive.
13. Need of sustenance.

Answers are on page 127.

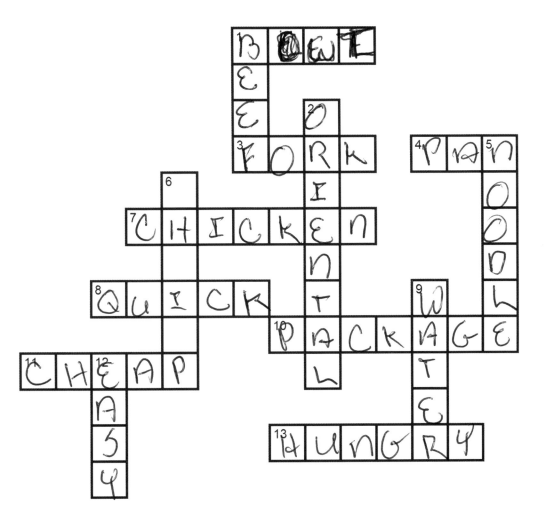

43

Popeye Cashew Ramen Salad

SALAD

2 packages ramen noodles (chicken flavor), seasoning packets removed and set aside

8 cups spinach leaves, torn

1½ cups diced cooked turkey or chicken

1 cup red or green grapes, halved

1 cup slivered red pepper

½ cup cashews, chopped

½ cup crumbled Gorgonzola or blue cheese

DRESSING

2 reserved seasoning packets

4 garlic cloves, minced

Juice of 1 small lemon

⅓ cup olive oil

¼ cup light mayonnaise

Red pepper rings and small grape clusters for garnish (optional)

1 Cook the noodles according to package directions.

2 Drain and cool, then cut the noodles up slightly.

3 In a large bowl, combine with other salad ingredients.

4 In a small bowl, mix the contents of the reserved seasoning packets, garlic, and lemon juice and let stand 15 minutes.

5 Add the oil and mayonnaise and whisk until smooth.

6 Pour the dressing over the salad and toss until thoroughly mixed.

7 Garnish if desired and serve.

WHAT YOU'RE GONNA DO!

When did you serve this dish for the first time?

_____

_____

Did you share the dish?

_____

_____

Whom did you share it with?

_____

_____

What was the occasion?

_____

_____

What did you serve with it?

_____

_____

Any special memories of the dish/activities?

_____

_____

How would you rate this dish?

_____

_____

Comments:

_____

_____

Easy Cheesy Ramen

SERVES 2

1 package ramen noodles (any flavor), seasoning packet removed and set aside

1 cup sour cream

1 cup grated Swiss cheese

2 ounces Parmesan cheese, grated

½ cup sweet-hot mustard or to taste

1 Cook the noodles according to package directions. Drain well.

2 Add the contents of the reserved seasoning packet and mix well.

3 Add the sour cream, Swiss cheese, and Parmesan cheese.

4 Mix completely.

5 Add the mustard and serve.

WHAT YOU'RE GONNA DO!

When did you serve this dish for the first time?

_____

_____

Did you share the dish?

_____

_____

Whom did you share it with?

_____

_____

What was the occasion?

_____

_____

What did you serve with it?

_____

_____

Any special memories of the dish/activities?

_____

_____

How would you rate this dish?

_____

_____

Comments:

_____

_____

Fit-for-a-King Salad

SERVES 4

2 packages ramen noodles (garden vegetable flavor), seasoning packets removed and set aside

2 cups shredded red or green cabbage

4 green onions, chopped

2 tablespoons sesame seeds

½ cup drained canned mandarin orange slices

1 cup shredded carrots

2 tablespoons shelled unsalted sunflower seeds

⅓ cup sugar

⅓ cup light vegetable oil

½ teaspoon mustard powder

Salt and freshly ground black pepper to taste

Juice of 1 fresh lime

½ cup slivered almonds or pine nuts

½ cup grated provolone cheese

1 Cook the noodles according to package directions. Drain well.

2 Place the noodles in large salad bowl.

3 Add the cabbage, onions, sesame seeds, orange slices, carrots, and sunflower seeds and toss.

4 In a mixing cup, combine the sugar, oil, mustard powder, salt, pepper, lime juice, and the contents of one of the reserved seasoning packets.

5 Mix well and then add to noodle mixture.

6 Just before serving, sprinkle with the nuts and cheese.

WHAT YOU'RE GONNA DO!

When did you serve this dish for the first time?

_____

_____

Did you share the dish?

_____

_____

Whom did you share it with?

_____

_____

What was the occasion?

_____

_____

What did you serve with it?

_____

_____

Any special memories of the dish/activities?

_____

_____

How would you rate this dish?

_____

_____

Comments:

_____

_____

Four-Alarm Fish Ramen

3 cups water

1 teaspoon Ginger-Garlic Paste (see Note opposite)

1 package ramen noodles (any flavor), seasoning packet removed and set aside

2 pieces breaded fish fillets

½ cup frozen mixed Chinese stirfry vegetables

1 teaspoon sesame oil

Chili powder to taste

1 green onion, thinly sliced for garnish

1 teaspoon sesame seeds, toasted for garnish

1 Bring the water to a boil.

2 Add the Ginger-Garlic Paste and ramen noodles; cook according to package directions.

3 While the noodles are cooking prepare the fish fillets according to their package directions.

4 Add the contents of the reserved seasoning packet and mixed stirfry vegetables to the noodles.

5 Cook 2 minutes then remove from heat.

6 Add the sesame oil and pour into a large bowl.

7 Sprinkle with the chili powder and stir.

8 Place the cooked fish on top.

9 Garnish with the green onion and sesame seeds and serve immediately.

Note: Ginger-Garlic Paste: Mix 2 inches fresh ginger, cut into slices, with 6 to 8 garlic cloves in a food processor. (Put the rest in your refrigerator for later use.)

WHAT YOU'RE GONNA DO!

When did you serve this dish for the first time?

_____

_____

Did you share the dish?

_____

_____

Whom did you share it with?

_____

_____

What was the occasion?

_____

_____

What did you serve with it?

_____

_____

Any special memories of the dish/activities?

_____

_____

How would you rate this dish?

_____

_____

Comments:

_____

_____

RAMEN
LORE

Being from a family where men don't cook, my first experiments in cooking were in college and involved ramen, garlic, and onions. From there I branched out, became more inquisitive. What else could I mix with ramen? Carrots, Brussels sprouts, lima beans, even meat. I ate some tough assortments, but I can now whip up a spaghetti sauce with whatever is on hand. Thanks, ramen!

—MINDSCI

RAMEN
FACTOIDS
ALERT
№ 3

If all the ramen noodles consumed by Americans in one day were stacked on top of each other, they would probably fall over.

Orange "PEZ" Chicken Soup

SERVES 4

1 package ramen noodles (chicken flavor), seasoning packet removed and set aside

4 dried hot peppers, the hotter the better

2 tablespoons Worcestershire or soy sauce

5 packs "Pez," orange, divided use

4 cups cooked rice (fried or white rice)

1 Cook the noodles according to package directions. Add the hot peppers to the water.

2 Remove the peppers after they're cooked. (Optional, but it's highly recommended.)

3 Add the Worcestershire sauce and all but two "Pez" pieces to the noodles. Make sure the "Pez" dissolves.

4 Mix the noodles and broth with the cooked rice.

5 Add the contents of the reserved seasoning packet to the mixture and stir.

6 Serve with a garnish of the reserved "Pez."

WHAT YOU'RE GONNA DO!

When did you serve this dish for the first time?

_____

_____

Did you share the dish?

_____

_____

Whom did you share it with?

_____

_____

What was the occasion?

_____

_____

What did you serve with it?

_____

_____

Any special memories of the dish/activities?

_____

_____

How would you rate this dish?

_____

_____

Comments:

_____

_____

Thai-One-On Ramen

SERVES 4

2 tablespoons vegetable oil

Garlic

2 packages ramen noodles (beef flavor)

2 boiled chicken breasts, cut into small cubes

1 shot sake

Soy sauce

Juice of 2 to 4 lemons

Bean sprouts to taste

Cilantro leaves to taste

Celery leaves

1 head iceberg lettuce, chopped

Red pepper flakes to taste

1 Chop the garlic and sauté until golden brown in the oil.

2 Once the garlic is sautéed, put it in a jar with a lid and cover with the oil.

3 Cook the noodles according to package directions. Drain well.

4 Spoon into a bowl.

5 Mix into the bowl the following: the chicken, sake, 10 shakes of soy sauce, 2 teaspoons of lemon juice, bean sprouts, cilantro leaves, celery leaves, lettuce, and red pepper flakes.

6 Add ¼ teaspoon of drained garlic.

7 Stir and taste. The taste should be a little, or a lot, hot, sour, and crunchy.

8 Garnish with a bean sprout and serve.

WHAT YOU'RE GONNA DO!

When did you serve this dish for the first time?

_____

_____

Did you share the dish?

_____

_____

Whom did you share it with?

_____

_____

What was the occasion?

_____

_____

What did you serve with it?

_____

_____

Any special memories of the dish/activities?

_____

_____

How would you rate this dish?

_____

_____

Comments:

_____

_____

Rip-Roaring Ramen Chili

SERVES 4

1 package ramen noodles (beef flavor)

1 pound hamburger

2 cans chili beans

2 cans tomatoes

2 chopped jalapeños

1 white onion, chopped

1 teaspoon cinnamon

1 Cook the noodles according to package directions.

2 Fry the hamburger and drain.

3 Put the beans, tomatoes, hamburger, jalapeños, onion, and cinnamon in a saucepan.

4 Slowly bring to a boil.

5 Stir in the ramen noodles and broth.

6 Remove from the heat.

7 Serve with peanut butter sandwich.

WHAT YOU'RE GONNA DO!

When did you serve this dish for the first time?
_____
_____

Did you share the dish?
_____
_____

Whom did you share it with?
_____
_____

What was the occasion?
_____
_____

What did you serve with it?
_____
_____

Any special memories of the dish/activities?
_____
_____

How would you rate this dish?
_____
_____

Comments:
_____
_____

RAMEN
LORE

When I was a kid, I used to bring ramen to school.
I would pour the flavoring on the uncooked noodles
and eat them. A lot of the kids did this, until one day
someone started a rumor that you could get worms
eating them that way. From then on we were not allowed
to do that at school. I still wonder who had made up
that story.

—ELAIDA T.

Ramen Word Scramble

1. LKRSINEP _ _ _ _ _ _ _ _
2. LMDI   milo
3. MAH   ham
4. ASASUGE   sausage
5. PSOON   spoon
6. LDASA   salad
7. NLOEODS   noodles
8. OFOD   food
9. DNSSGEIR   Dersing _ _ _
10. CNZAUHES _ _ _ _ _ _ _ _
11. ERHRYS   SHERRY
12. EORKAN
13. FOZENR   FROZEN
14. RCUNHB   Brunch
15. DIRNNE   Dinner
16. OSY   soy

17. OENHY   Honey
18. BNGAIK   BAKING
19. EMEMIORS   memoirs
20. PCHAE   Cheap
21. HLNUC   Lunch
22. GMERANRAI   MARGARINE
23. STKAE   STEAK
24. LOI   Oil
25. RADNIED   DRAINED
26. EEPPPR   PEPPER
27. OASCRTR   CARROTS
28. OLBI   Boil
29. TTESA   TASTE
30. ANARSMEP   PARMESAN
31. ICKHNCE   CHICKEN
32. PCEATK _ _ _ _ _ _

Answers are on page 128.

61

Odds-and-Ends Hearty Ramen Soup

1 package ramen noodles (any flavor, broken up)

1 (16-ounce) can cream-style corn

¼ teaspoon powdered ginger

¼ teaspoon curry powder

¼ teaspoon onion powder

¼ teaspoon garlic powder

½ cup milk or soy milk, or more if needed

½ cup grated Cheddar cheese

Pinch salt and freshly ground black pepper

2 parsley sprigs for garnish

1 Cook the noodles according to package directions. Drain well.

2 Mix in the cream-style corn, ginger, curry, onion powder, garlic powder, and milk.

3 Heat over medium heat. If using real milk, don't let the soup boil.

4 When all the ingredients are heated through, add the grated cheese.

5 Mix until the cheese melts.

6 Add the salt and pepper to taste. Adjust the consistency with more milk if the soup is too thick.

7 Garnish each serving with a sprig of parsley and serve.

WHAT YOU'RE GONNA DO!

When did you serve this dish for the first time?

_____

_____

Did you share the dish?

_____

_____

Whom did you share it with?

_____

_____

What was the occasion?

_____

_____

What did you serve with it?

_____

_____

Any special memories of the dish/activities?

_____

_____

How would you rate this dish?

_____

_____

Comments:

_____

_____

Hawaiian Chicken Ramen

SERVES 2

2 packages ramen noodles (chicken flavor), seasoning packets removed and set aside

1 egg, beaten

2 cups sliced chicken breasts

1 teaspoon sesame oil

1 cup chopped red pepper

1 cup broccoli florets

1 (8-ounce) can crushed pineapple in syrup

1 tablespoon sugar

1 tablespoon vinegar

2 teaspoons cornstarch

Broccoli florets and red pepper for garnish

1 Preheat the oven to 350°.

2 Cook the noodles according to package directions. Drain well.

3 Mix in the beaten egg.

4 Place half of the noodles in the bottom of a pie plate.

5 Sauté the chicken in the sesame oil for 5 minutes.

6 Add the red pepper and broccoli florets. Sauté for 3 additional minutes.

7 Stir in the contents of the reserved seasoning packets, pineapple and juice, sugar, vinegar, and cornstarch.

8 Cook 3 to 5 minutes until thickened.

9 Place the chicken mixture on the noodles in the pie plate.

10 Top with remaining noodles and bake for 20 minutes.

11 Garnish with the broccoli and red pepper and serve.

WHAT YOU'RE GONNA DO!

When did you serve this dish for the first time?

_____

_____

Did you share the dish?

_____

_____

Whom did you share it with?

_____

_____

What was the occasion?

_____

_____

What did you serve with it?

_____

_____

Any special memories of the dish/activities?

_____

_____

How would you rate this dish?

_____

_____

Comments:

_____

_____

Big Shrimp Omelets

1 cup finely chopped celery

1 cup finely chopped green onions

1 cup finely chopped tiny shrimp or small shrimp

3 tablespoons oil

3 tablespoons soy sauce

⅓ teaspoon ginger

1 package ramen noodles (shrimp flavor)

1¼ cups boiling water

3 eggs

4 sprigs of fresh parsley

1 Sauté the celery, onions, and shrimp in the oil. Add the soy sauce and ginger.

2 At the same time, begin preparing the ramen noodles, using only the 1¼ cups of boiling water.

3 Cook the noodles only 2 to 3 minutes with seasoning packet.

4 Beat the eggs until pale yellow; set aside.

5 Let the sautéed mixture cool.

6 Stir the ramen to break up the noodles. Drain well.

7 Add the sautéed mixture with the liquid to the noodles.

8 Stir the ingredients until everything is well coated.

9 Add the beaten eggs.

10 Pour a thin layer of vegetable oil into a small frying pan. When the oil is hot, spoon the ramen mixture into the pan to make 4-inch omelets.

11 Fry until golden brown on both sides.

12 Garnish with the fresh parsley.

WHAT YOU'RE GONNA DO!

When did you serve this dish for the first time?

_____

_____

Did you share the dish?

_____

_____

Whom did you share it with?

_____

_____

What was the occasion?

_____

_____

What did you serve with it?

_____

_____

Any special memories of the dish/activities?

_____

_____

How would you rate this dish?

_____

_____

Comments:

_____

_____

Rootin' Tootin' Ramen Chili

SERVES 4

3 packages ramen noodles, seasoning packets removed

3 jalapeño peppers, diced

1 can chili

1½ cups shredded cheese (Monterey Jack works best)

3 tablespoons hot sauce

1 Cook the noodles and jalapeño together according to package directions.

2 Pour it into a large bowl.

3 Add the chili and cheese.

4 Microwave on high until the cheese is melted.

5 Stir.

6 Add the hot sauce to taste and serve.

WHAT YOU'RE GONNA DO!

When did you serve this dish for the first time?

_____

_____

Did you share the dish?

_____

_____

Whom did you share it with?

_____

_____

What was the occasion?

_____

_____

What did you serve with it?

_____

_____

Any special memories of the dish/activities?

_____

_____

How would you rate this dish?

_____

_____

Comments:

_____

_____

Cholesterol-Killer Ramen

SERVES 1

1 package ramen noodles (any flavor), seasoning packet removed and set aside

5 tablespoons margarine or butter

Cumin to taste

Generous amount sesame seeds, toasted (see Variation opposite)

1 Cook the noodles according to package directions. Drain well.

2 Add the margarine and stir until melted.

3 Add the contents of the reserved seasoning packet, sprinkle with the cumin, and stir well.

4 If the noodles seem too dry at this point, add a dash of hot water and stir.

5 Place the noodles in a serving bowl.

6 Add toasted sesame seeds to the top of the noodles as a garnish and serve.

Variation: For variety, garnish this with a dollop of mayonnaise.

WHAT YOU'RE GONNA DO!

When did you serve this dish for the first time?

_____

_____

Did you share the dish?

_____

_____

Whom did you share it with?

_____

_____

What was the occasion?

_____

_____

What did you serve with it?

_____

_____

Any special memories of the dish/activities?

_____

_____

How would you rate this dish?

_____

_____

Comments:

_____

_____

Ramen Word Search

ramen	sausage	sauce	packet
chicken	pour	Pez	frozen
spoon	mild	rice	boil
pasta	baking	scallions	cheese
flavor	oriental	Parmesan	garlic
mushrooms	margarine	tomato	fork
sherry	corn	college	leftover
kimche	drained	fish	cheap
mix	spinach	seasoning	lunch
sprinkle	Korean	carrots	sesame
noodles	hamburger	taste	dressing
beef	Szechuan	ham	cups
Elvis	honey	soy	steak
salad	food	water	onion
tuna	shrimp	tortillas	egg
tofu	toasted	memories	brunch
pepper	peas	dinner	

Answers are on page 129.

```
D E L X K C D V O X U K U C Q C Q V W L P A Y H M T T L X Q L N
L S L I Z K Q G E S E I R O M E M J Y B B E U D G H J M M A E J
Q A Z G J V S C A L L I O N S V K W O E T O P P B U S N R Z N H
W B B A N U T C Q Z Q P V G V Q A R A F N U H Q J H D Z A D A U
G Q O D L I M U D M H H A M N T S B O S A Q T R E B O B X E S S
K Z V I T L F W D E J E A J E I W E N F P X H R P Q O Y R G E Q
N U X F L O B T W B T D Q R A T N U T Z L I R G A D F F J E M I
F L V X T F L A V O R S R S O T C O R S K Y N V V J A F P L R C
A A J V T X N W N O K L A A P N S S U A W X A L X I F K L A L
Q Z B D R A I N E D M O X O P O F A A A A T P O C S R W S O P T
C H A M B U R G E R C O R Y T E O W P T E O A P H H B I A C V Q
Z B F P H M D B S T E A K K F H P N J G U S N I J K V H N T Q K
F Q N N K E E F L E F T O V E R Y K S R P N S A L L I T R O T D
J R G S Q E M X W F M R C N O E W E N E Z O R F E N Y C S Q G D
K J J A F F B A X X D E I B O S N V M J L U N C H X Y W W R V X
E Y S E N Q P G S L V R R K M P Y P Q S M L B F R I R A M E N A
Y Y Q P O X U Q E E A R A E D R K I S I U M D R E S S I N G P E
I U S Q O H Z O U G S W O Q N F W J S O T A M O T G V C H Y H
Z T A X D E S I R U N V D B F N U Y X D G O D O H B S G C F J C
G R V N L G D A S O G S D K E K I C Q D D K E Z R W N T Z X R K
E P J G E A M V U M I B S Z Z L V D G O W N V R R F N N H B K E
Q N S C S S D C V I O U J X N E B T L A S R E U A C S K Y M Q C
S E L Y U U C X Z U L O J I I J A P X Z Z Z V E G G T X K K O J
F S J C N A Z I J P N C R T U M K T B K E H G K G O O Y X A N I
W E B I M S X A I S M E E H C W O L T C I F J Q R R U I K H
L E P M I R H S V V P K R I S C N E H R H H S T U I R S O Y O D
L H U H W Y T K F C G S Y U G C C Z U U C R M E A P A G N Q
Q C Z W O B R S E A V M A G E P M U Y X A V X C L N C P J L T I
L B W I O T B P P D K C R R W S R A B U N X F Q M T J A H N A F
L P K O R E A N L Y Q H L Y B C I S I P F J V D X A L E K J M D
E H B E C O R N A O K E I T Q L C C F B F W R F F L G H T Y E S
C C H I C K E N B X A D C V W Z E L I B H C N U R B F C Z E P R
```

Elvis's Fav' Gravy Ramen

SERVES 2

1 package ramen noodles, seasoning packet removed and set aside

3 tablespoons dried onion flakes

2 tablespoons vegetable oil

1 tablespoon browning sauce

1½ tablespoons flour

1 cup cold water

1 Cook the noodles according to package directions.

2 Sauté the contents of the reserved seasoning packet and onion flakes in the oil.

3 Add the browning sauce.

4 In a small bowl, mix the flour with 1 cup cold water.

5 Slowly add the flour mixture to the browning sauce mixture, stirring constantly.

6 Cook on medium heat until thickened to make the gravy.

7 Pour the gravy over the noodles and serve.

WHAT YOU'RE GONNA DO!

When did you serve this dish for the first time?

_____

_____

Did you share the dish?

_____

_____

Whom did you share it with?

_____

_____

What was the occasion?

_____

_____

What did you serve with it?

_____

_____

Any special memories of the dish/activities?

_____

_____

How would you rate this dish?

_____

_____

Comments:

_____

_____

Porky's Stir-Fry

6 ounces boneless pork, cut into strips (see Note opposite)

Soy sauce

Freshly ground black pepper to taste

Vegetable oil

Pinch sugar (optional)

2 packages ramen noodles (oriental flavor)

2 tablespoons margarine

1 Marinate the pork strips in the soy sauce and pepper.

2 Heat a skillet until hot and add enough vegetable oil to coat the bottom of the pan.

3 Add the pork and cook until done, stirring constantly.

4 Add a pinch of sugar (if using it) to the pork and cook just long enough to melt the sugar.

5 Cook the noodles according to package directions and break up the noodles.

6 Drain the noodles and leave slightly wet.

7 Add the margarine to the noodles and stir well.

8 Add the pork and stir well.

9 Divide into two portions and serve.

Note: This can also be made with chicken and beef, but omit the soy sauce and sugar.

WHAT YOU'RE GONNA DO!

When did you serve this dish for the first time?

_____

_____

Did you share the dish?

_____

_____

Whom did you share it with?

_____

_____

What was the occasion?

_____

_____

What did you serve with it?

_____

_____

Any special memories of the dish/activities?

_____

_____

How would you rate this dish?

_____

_____

Comments:

_____

_____

Top-Speed 3-Minute Ramen

SERVES 1

1 package ramen noodles (chicken flavor)

1 jalapeño pepper, sliced

1 to 2 green onions, sliced

1 to 2 radishes, sliced

1 Cook the noodles according to package directions (see Note below).

2 Add the pepper, onion, and radish to the noodles during last minute of boiling.

3 Mix well and serve.

Note: Drain off 1 cup of water before adding the flavor packet.

WHAT YOU'RE GONNA DO!

When did you serve this dish for the first time?

_____

_____

Did you share the dish?

_____

_____

Whom did you share it with?

_____

_____

What was the occasion?

_____

_____

What did you serve with it?

_____

_____

Any special memories of the dish/activities?

_____

_____

How would you rate this dish?

_____

_____

Comments:

_____

_____

Crabby Spinach Ramen

SERVES 2

2 packages ramen noodles (any flavor)

1 (12-ounce) package imitation crabmeat

1 (14-ounce) can spinach

Salt and freshly ground black pepper

1 Cook the noodles according to package directions.

2 Add the crabmeat and spinach; do not drain.

3 Bring back to a boil to heat the meat and spinach through.

4 Add salt and pepper to taste.

5 Drain and serve.

WHAT YOU'RE GONNA DO!

When did you serve this dish for the first time?

_____

_____

Did you share the dish?

_____

_____

Whom did you share it with?

_____

_____

What was the occasion?

_____

_____

What did you serve with it?

_____

_____

Any special memories of the dish/activities?

_____

_____

How would you rate this dish?

_____

_____

Comments:

_____

_____

Ramen Cookie Delight

1 package ramen noodles (chicken flavor), seasoning packet removed and set aside

4 semoa cookies (see Note opposite)

Salt and freshly ground black pepper

1 Crush the ramen noodles.

2 Crush the cookies.

3 Mix the cookies into the ramen noodles.

4 Add the contents of the reserved seasoning packet.

5 Salt and pepper to taste and serve.

Note: You can buy these by name in any store. You can also buy Girl Scout cookies known as Caramel Delights, which are semoa cookies.

WHAT YOU'RE GONNA DO!

When did you serve this dish for the first time?

_____

_____

Did you share the dish?

_____

_____

Whom did you share it with?

_____

_____

What was the occasion?

_____

_____

What did you serve with it?

_____

_____

Any special memories of the dish/activities?

_____

_____

How would you rate this dish?

_____

_____

Comments:

_____

_____

Pseudo Szechwan Ramen

SERVES 2

1 package ramen noodles (hot and spicy or pork flavor), seasoning packet removed and set aside

1 small onion, finely diced

½ cup finely diced chicken, beef, pork, or Spam

¼ cup frozen peas

1 tablespoon Szechwan sauce

1 Cook the noodles according to package directions. Drain well. Set aside.

2 Sauté the onion and meat until the onion is transparent and the meat is slightly browned.

3 Cook the peas according to package instructions.

4 Add the noodles and the peas to the meat mixture and heat through.

5 Stir in half the contents of the reserved seasoning packet and the Szechwan sauce and serve.

WHAT YOU'RE GONNA DO!

When did you serve this dish for the first time?

_____

_____

Did you share the dish?

_____

_____

Whom did you share it with?

_____

_____

What was the occasion?

_____

_____

What did you serve with it?

_____

_____

Any special memories of the dish/activities?

_____

_____

How would you rate this dish?

_____

_____

Comments:

_____

_____

Saturday Brunch Ramen

2½ cups water

1 package ramen noodles (oriental flavor), seasoning packet removed and set aside

¼ cup frozen corn

1 beaten egg

Leftover chicken, ham, or pork chop, diced

Freshly ground black pepper

1 Bring the water to a boil.

2 Add the contents of the reserved seasoning packet, corn, and noodles.

3 When noodles are nearly done, stir in the egg quickly so you don't get lumps of boiled egg. Simmer for 1 minute.

4 Add the chicken or ham or the pork chop. Toss gently. Sprinkle with the freshly ground pepper and serve.

WHAT YOU'RE GONNA DO!

When did you serve this dish for the first time?

_____

_____

Did you share the dish?

_____

_____

Whom did you share it with?

_____

_____

What was the occasion?

_____

_____

What did you serve with it?

_____

_____

Any special memories of the dish/activities?

_____

_____

How would you rate this dish?

_____

_____

Comments:

_____

_____

RAMEN
LORE

Once I had to ship a glass to my brother (in a hurry, too).
I had gotten everything ready to go and I was about to
add the packing peanuts, when I realized I forgot to buy
some. In a frenzy I searched my cabinets for something
to use for packing. When I opened my cupboard I saw
I had a good supply of ramen noodles. So I broke up
the packages and used them as filler for the package.
The glass arrived safely at my brother's house a few days
later! Thanks a bunch, ramen!

—DAN H.

RAMEN
FACTOIDS
ALERT
№ 4

It would take 432,000
packages of ramen noodles
to cover a football field.

Then pray it doesn't rain.

Kickin' Dduk-Boki

SERVES 2

1 package frozen Korean rice cakes

2 tablespoons red pepper paste

1 tablespoon soy sauce

1 green onion, chopped

1 tablespoon sesame seed oil

1 garlic clove, minced

1 package ramen noodles (any flavor)

Sesame seeds

1 Add the Korean rice cakes to enough boiling water to cook until soft.

2 Discard all but ½ cup boiling water.

3 Add the pepper paste, soy sauce, green onion, sesame seed oil, minced garlic, and uncooked ramen noodles with the seasoning packet.

4 Mix until the noodles soften; you may leave the noodles hard if you prefer.

5 Sprinkle the sesame seeds over and serve.

WHAT YOU'RE GONNA DO!

When did you serve this dish for the first time?

_____

_____

Did you share the dish?

_____

_____

Whom did you share it with?

_____

_____

What was the occasion?

_____

_____

What did you serve with it?

_____

_____

Any special memories of the dish/activities?

_____

_____

How would you rate this dish?

_____

_____

Comments:

_____

_____

Hog 'n' Cheese Mix and Melt

SERVES 1

1 package ramen noodles (any flavor)

4 American cheese slices

1 cooked ham steak

1 Cook the noodles according to package directions using half the contents of the seasoning packet.

2 Drain the noodles and place them in a bowl.

3 Cut the cheese and ham into small chunks and add them to the hot noodles.

4 Cover the bowl and let it sit until the cheese melts, approximately 5 minutes. Stir to mix and serve.

WHAT YOU'RE GONNA DO!

When did you serve this dish for the first time?

_____

_____

Did you share the dish?

_____

_____

Whom did you share it with?

_____

_____

What was the occasion?

_____

_____

What did you serve with it?

_____

_____

Any special memories of the dish/activities?

_____

_____

How would you rate this dish?

_____

_____

Comments:

_____

_____

Poppin' Broccoli Slaw

1 package ramen noodles (any flavor), seasoning packet removed

1 bottle poppy seed salad dressing

2 tablespoons vinegar

1 package broccoli slaw

1 Cook the noodles according to package directions.

2 Toss together all the ingredients.

3 Refrigerate 2 hours and serve.

WHAT YOU'RE GONNA DO!

When did you serve this dish for the first time?

_____

_____

Did you share the dish?

_____

_____

Whom did you share it with?

_____

_____

What was the occasion?

_____

_____

What did you serve with it?

_____

_____

Any special memories of the dish/activities?

_____

_____

How would you rate this dish?

_____

_____

Comments:

_____

_____

Buttery Sesame Ramen

1 package ramen noodles (any flavor), seasoning packet removed and set aside

2 teaspoons margarine or butter

Dash cumin

Generous amount toasted sesame seeds

1 Cook the noodles according to package directions.

2 Add the margarine.

3 Stir in one-half to three-quarters of the contents of the reserved seasoning packet.

4 Sprinkle with the cumin.

5 Place the mixture in serving bowl.

6 Sprinkle the toasted sesame seeds over and serve.

Variation: For variety, garnish with a dollop of mayonnaise.

WHAT YOU'RE GONNA DO!

When did you serve this dish for the first time?
_____
_____

Did you share the dish?
_____
_____

Whom did you share it with?
_____
_____

What was the occasion?
_____
_____

What did you serve with it?
_____
_____

Any special memories of the dish/activities?
_____
_____

How would you rate this dish?
_____
_____

Comments:
_____
_____

Cheap-as-It-Gets Ramen Salad

¼ cup frozen corn

¼ cup frozen peas

1 package ramen noodles (any flavor)

¼ cup sliced carrots

Creamy Italian salad dressing

1 Cook the corn and peas according to package directions. Drain and chill.

2 Cook the noodles according to package directions.

3 Drain the noodles then run under cold water to cool. Drain well.

4 Add the vegetables and the salad dressing to taste.

5 Toss lightly and serve.

WHAT YOU'RE GONNA DO!

When did you serve this dish for the first time?

_____

_____

Did you share the dish?

_____

_____

Whom did you share it with?

_____

_____

What was the occasion?

_____

_____

What did you serve with it?

_____

_____

Any special memories of the dish/activities?

_____

_____

How would you rate this dish?

_____

_____

Comments:

_____

_____

Death Valley Treat

SERVES 6

6 cups water

1 can corn, drained

1 can peas, drained

1 can chicken or tuna, drained

3 packages ramen noodles (beef, chicken, or oriental flavor)

Hot sauce to taste

1 Bring the water to a boil.

2 Add the corn, peas, and chicken or tuna and boil for 1 minute.

3 Add the noodles and the contents of the seasoning packets. Lower the heat and simmer until the noodles are done.

4 Add the hot sauce, mix to combine, and serve.

WHAT YOU'RE GONNA DO!

When did you serve this dish for the first time?

_____

_____

Did you share the dish?

_____

_____

Whom did you share it with?

_____

_____

What was the occasion?

_____

_____

What did you serve with it?

_____

_____

Any special memories of the dish/activities?

_____

_____

How would you rate this dish?

_____

_____

Comments:

_____

_____

RAMEN
LORE

The first time I ever had ramen noodles, I thought I was eating something that was Korean. My brother had come home on leave from Korea—where he was posted in the Army—and he had brought some with him. He said it was his favorite thing to eat in Korea. I am not sure if they were available in the U.S. at that time, but I sure loved the taste and never forgot my first bowl. This was back in 1978.

—CUSSETA L.

Ramen Anagram Game

Using at least two letters of the word **ramen**, how many words
can you make? We came up with eighteen!

men	AMEN
mar	
near	
ram	
mean	
name	
namer	
arm	
an	
ran	
ear	
are	
era	
earn	

Answers are on page 127.

Florentine
à la Polo
and Newman

SERVES 2 TO 4

2 packages ramen noodles (any flavor), seasoning packets removed and set aside

1 small box frozen chopped spinach

1 small can mushrooms

1 block semisoft tofu

Italian salad dressing

1 Cook the noodles according to package directions. Drain well.

2 Add the contents of the flavor packets.

3 Break up the spinach and add to the noodles.

4 Mix in the mushrooms and tofu.

5 Add just enough salad dressing to coat, then gently toss and serve.

WHAT YOU'RE GONNA DO!

When did you serve this dish for the first time?

_____

_____

Did you share the dish?

_____

_____

Whom did you share it with?

_____

_____

What was the occasion?

_____

_____

What did you serve with it?

_____

_____

Any special memories of the dish/activities?

_____

_____

How would you rate this dish?

_____

_____

Comments:

_____

_____

Hijacked Taco Bell Ramen

Two stalks celery, diced

1 medium onion, diced

1½ cups diced cooked shrimp, chicken, or pork

1 tablespoon cooking oil

Dash soy sauce

Pinch of ginger

1 package ramen noodles (any flavor)

10 packages Taco Bell Mild Sauce (see Note opposite)

2 eggs

Fresh parsley, for garnish

1 Sauté the celery, onions, and shrimp, chicken, or pork in the oil, adding the soy sauce and ginger.

2 At the same time, begin preparing the ramen noodles, using only 1½ cups water.

3 Cook the noodles only 2 to 3 minutes with seasoning packet and hot sauce packs.

4 Beat the eggs until pale yellow; set aside.

5 Let the sautéed mixture cool.

6 Stir the ramen to break up the noodles; drain well.

7 Add the sautéed mixture with its liquid to the noodles.

8 Stir the ingredients until everything is well coated.

9 Add the beaten eggs.

10 Spoon the mixture into a hot pan to make 4-inch omelets.

11 Fry until golden brown on both sides.

12 Garnish with the fresh parsley.

Note: If you ask the Taco Bell staff nicely they may give you some.

WHAT YOU'RE GONNA DO!

When did you serve this dish for the first time?

_____

_____

Did you share the dish?

_____

_____

Whom did you share it with?

_____

_____

What was the occasion?

_____

_____

What did you serve with it?

_____

_____

Any special memories of the dish/activities?

_____

_____

How would you rate this dish?

_____

_____

Comments:

_____

_____

Super Pregnancy Ramen

SERVES 1 TO 2

1 egg

2 cups water

1 package ramen noodles (sesame flavor), seasoning packet removed and set aside

3 tablespoons thinly sliced carrots

Sesame seed–nori mix (optional, see Note opposite)

2 tablespoons chopped scallions

1 Stir the egg with a fork.

2 Bring 2 cups water for the noodles to a boil. When the water boils, add the egg and carrots to the water with the noodles.

3 Cook the noodles until they are soft.

4 Drain off all but a small amount of the water.

5 To the bottom of a serving bowl, add the contents of the reserved seasoning packet, nori mix, and scallions. Stir together.

6 Pour the noodles in the bowl, mix, and serve.

Note: Crushed sesame seed–nori mix is available in Japanese markets.

WHAT YOU'RE GONNA DO!

When did you serve this dish for the first time?

_____

_____

Did you share the dish?

_____

_____

Whom did you share it with?

_____

_____

What was the occasion?

_____

_____

What did you serve with it?

_____

_____

Any special memories of the dish/activities?

_____

_____

How would you rate this dish?

_____

_____

Comments:

_____

_____

RAMEN
LORE

When I became pregnant for the first time most food smelled bad, looked bad, and tasted bad to me. Even when I was able to eat something it didn't stay down. Then I discovered ramen noodles. Finally, something that agreed with all my senses. Thanks, ramen, for keeping me from starving.

—SANDRA J.

RAMEN
LORE

When I was in school one of my friends told me a story about a ramen noodle experience he had. One night after a big party he came home and decided he needed a bath, since he was sore and sticky from the party. Well, he took his bath—and fell asleep in the tub. When he woke up, his bath was full of ramen noodles. It seems that his roommate had added the ramen noodles while he was passed out. He said that it was the freakiest thing to wake up in a tub of noodles. But the worst part was that, when he went to his kitchen to get some lunch and looked in his cabinet, all of his noodles were gone and he had no lunch.

—CHRIS H.

Custom Kimche Ramen-Style

¼ cup diced onion

¼ cup diced green pepper

Garlic to taste

Oil

2 cups water

1 package ramen noodles (any flavor)

½ cup kimche (available at any Japanese market)

1 tablespoon sesame oil

1 egg

½ cup cooked sausage or hamburger

1 Sauté the onion, pepper, and garlic in a small amount of oil until done.

2 Add 2 cups water and bring to a boil. Add the noodles and flavor packet.

3 When the noodles are almost done stir in the kimche.

4 Add the sesame oil. Heat to boiling.

5 Stir in the egg. When the egg is fully cooked remove the pan from the heat.

6 Stir in the cooked meat and serve.

WHAT YOU'RE GONNA DO!

When did you serve this dish for the first time?

_____

_____

Did you share the dish?

_____

_____

Whom did you share it with?

_____

_____

What was the occasion?

_____

_____

What did you serve with it?

_____

_____

Any special memories of the dish/activities?

_____

_____

How would you rate this dish?

_____

_____

Comments:

_____

_____

Super Ramen Burritos

1 package ramen noodles (chicken or beef flavor), seasoning packet removed and set aside

Hot sauce to taste

Parmesan cheese

2 flour tortillas

1 Cook the noodles according to package directions. Drain well.

2 Add the contents of the reserved seasoning packet, hot sauce, and Parmesan cheese.

3 Fold half the mixture into each tortilla and serve.

WHAT YOU'RE GONNA DO!

When did you serve this dish for the first time?

_____

_____

Did you share the dish?

_____

_____

Whom did you share it with?

_____

_____

What was the occasion?

_____

_____

What did you serve with it?

_____

_____

Any special memories of the dish/activities?

_____

_____

How would you rate this dish?

_____

_____

Comments:

_____

_____

RAMEN
FACTOIDS
ALERT
Nº 5

You can buy a new car for $20,000, or buy 167,667 packages of ramen noodles for the same $20,000.

Tough decision, no?

RAMEN
LORE

When I was a kid, we had Ichiban-brand ramen, and we called it "Itchy Bum noodles."

–J. STORMWOOD

During a really rough period in my life, I was basically flat broke. I had $9.00 to buy food for my daughter and me for the next two weeks. So I went and bought the basics: tuna, hot dogs, and lots of ramen noodles. Without the ramen noodles, we would have had food for only a couple of days. Thanks, ramen.

–GEORGIA T.

Red-Nosed Ramen

½ cup sherry cooking wine

2 cups water

2 packages ramen noodles (chicken flavor), seasoning packets removed and set aside

Cayenne pepper to taste

1 Pour the cooking sherry in the bottom of a pan.

2 Add the water and bring it to a boil.

3 Add one package of the noodles. (Save the other package for another recipe.)

4 When the noodles are done add the contents of both seasoning packets, stir, add pepper to taste, and serve.

WHAT YOU'RE GONNA DO!

When did you serve this dish for the first time?

_____

_____

Did you share the dish?

_____

_____

Whom did you share it with?

_____

_____

What was the occasion?

_____

_____

What did you serve with it?

_____

_____

Any special memories of the dish/activities?

_____

_____

How would you rate this dish?

_____

_____

Comments:

_____

_____

La Chico's Hearty Soup

SERVES 2

4 cups water

1 cup cubed cooked turkey or chicken

1 package ramen noodles (chicken flavor, see Step 2 opposite), seasoning packet removed and set aside

1 cup shredded lettuce

¼ cup chopped green onion

¼ cup thinly sliced radishes

½ cup chopped tomato

½ cup grated Monterey Jack cheese

Crushed oregano

Hot sauce

Warm tortillas or tortilla chips

1 Bring the water to a boil and add the turkey.

2 Break up the noodles before opening the package and add the broken ramen noodles to the water.

3 Cook 3 minutes.

4 Add the contents of the reserved seasoning packet.

5 Divide the soup between two bowls.

6 To each add half the lettuce, green onion, radishes, tomato, and cheese.

7 Sprinkle each bowl lightly with the crushed oregano and top the soup with some of your favorite hot sauce.

8 Serve with warm tortillas or tortilla chips.

WHAT YOU'RE GONNA DO!

When did you serve this dish for the first time?

_____

_____

Did you share the dish?

_____

_____

Whom did you share it with?

_____

_____

What was the occasion?

_____

_____

What did you serve with it?

_____

_____

Any special memories of the dish/activities?

_____

_____

How would you rate this dish?

_____

_____

Comments:

_____

_____

Vegetarian's Power Dish

4 tablespoons vegetable oil

1 onion, sliced and diced

1 red pepper, sliced and diced

1 yellow pepper, sliced and diced

1 orange pepper, sliced and diced

1 green pepper, sliced and diced

2 tomatoes, sliced and diced

1 teaspoon salt

½ teaspoon red chili powder

2 packages ramen noodles (any flavor), seasoning packets removed and set aside

4 tablespoons soy sauce

Black pepper to taste

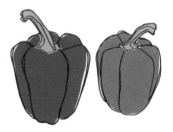

1 In a frying pan, add the oil, onion, peppers, and tomatoes.

2 Sauté on medium-high heat for 5 minutes.

3 Add the salt, pepper, chili powder, and seasoning packet; mix well.

4 Pour into a heatproof casserole dish or just a plain heatproof bowl.

5 Add the ramen noodles and soy sauce to the same pan.

6 Sauté on medium-high heat for 5 minutes.

7 Add the vegetables to the noodle mixture and toss together.

8 Sauté on high heat for 1 minute.

9 Remove from the heat and serve.

WHAT YOU'RE GONNA DO!

When did you serve this dish for the first time?

_____

_____

Did you share the dish?

_____

_____

Whom did you share it with?

_____

_____

What was the occasion?

_____

_____

What did you serve with it?

_____

_____

Any special memories of the dish/activities?

_____

_____

How would you rate this dish?

_____

_____

Comments:

_____

_____

RAMEN
LORE

One time when I was in college, I went on a fifty-mile
bike trip. On my arrival I rode to my friend's house to
get some rest and some food. When I got there, all he
had were two packages of ramen noodles. I whipped
those up just like the package told me to. They were the
most filling and satisfying things I have had in my life.
(At that time, that is.) They just happened to fill that void
on that day.

—TOM D.

RAMEN
LORE

She was a beef ramen masquerading as a chicken mushroom, but I was an experienced ramen hound and could sniff her out like a great dane on the hunt. Her saucy broth felt so hot on my tongue, slipping down my throat and dragging those perfectly shaped noodles behind it. The heat of our contact warmed me all over, I felt a rush of ecstasy . . . or was it the MSG?

—PUCK

(Is this guy right in the head?)

Answers

Answers to Ramen Crossword

Down
1. Beef
2. Oriental
5. Noodle
6. Shrimp
9. Water
12. Easy

Across
1. Bowl
3. Fork
4. Pan
7. Chicken
8. Quick
10. Package
11. Cheap
13. Hungry

Answers to Ramen Anagram Game

men	am	near
name	an	ear
are	ram	ran
mar	mare	ream
amen	arm	ma
man	mean	me

Answers to Ramen Word Scramble

1. LKRSINEP sprinkle
2. LMDI mild
3. MAH ham
4. ASASUGE sausage
5. PSOON spoon
6. LDASA salad
7. NLOEODS noodles
8. OFOD food
9. DNSSGEIR dressing
10. CNZAUHES Szechuan
11. ERHRYS sherry
12. EORKAN Korean
13. FOZENR frozen
14. RCUNHB brunch
15. DIRNNE dinner
16. OSY soy
17. OENHY honey
18. BNGAIK baking
19. EMEMIORS memories
20. PCHAE cheap
21. HLNUC lunch
22. GMERANRAI margarine
23. STKAE steak
24. LOI oil
25. RADNIED drained
26. EEPPPR pepper
27. OASCRTR carrots
28. OLBI boil
29. TTESA taste
30. ANARSMEP Parmesan
31. ICKHNCE chicken
32. PCEATK packet

Answers to Ramen Word Search

EVERYBODY LOVES RAMEN

Andrews McMeel Publishing
a division of Andrews McMeel Universal
1130 Walnut Street, Kansas City, Missouri 64106

www.andrewsmcmeel.com

16 17 18 19 20 TEN 10 9 8 7 6 5 4 3 2 1

ISBN: 978-1-4494-7893-3

Library of Congress Control Number: 2016931062

Editor: Patty Rice
Art Director: Holly Ogden
Illustrations: Brenna Thummler
Production Manager: Tamara Haus
Production Editor: Grace Bornhoft